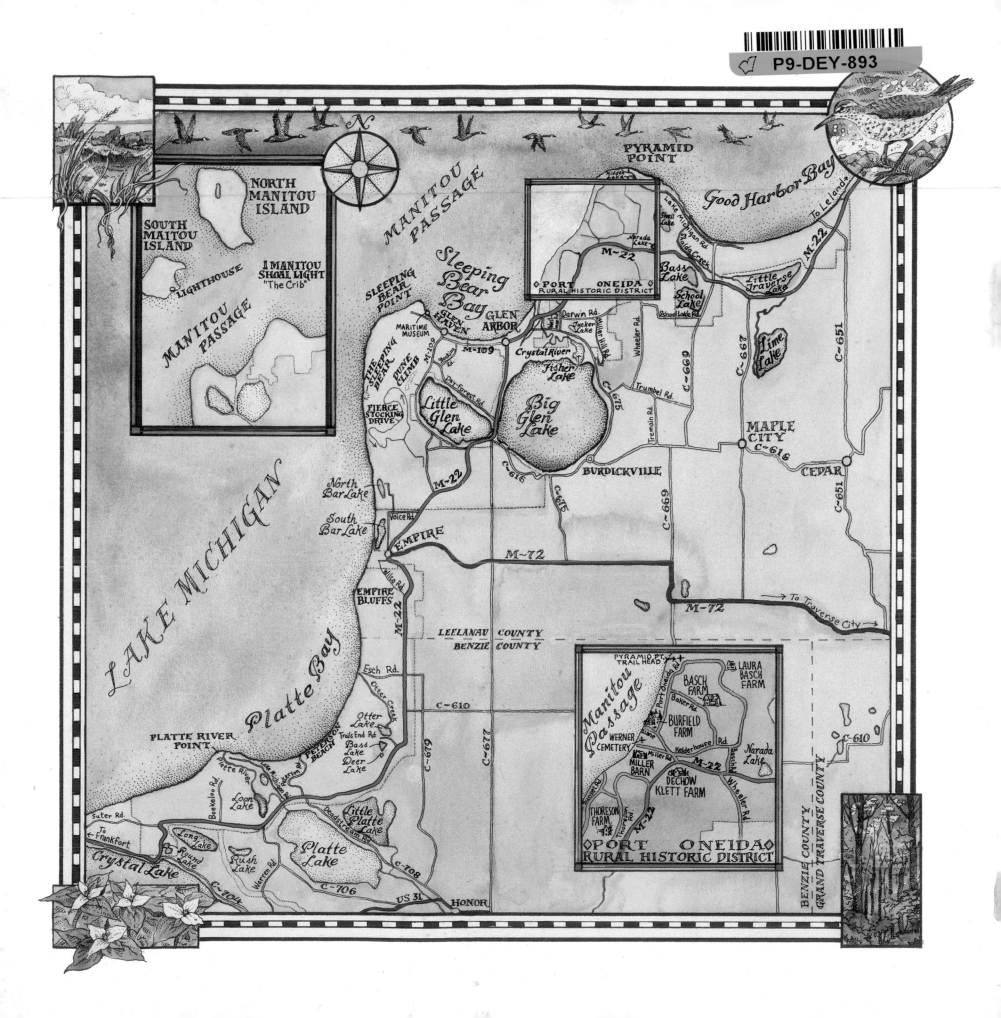

NORTH
MANITOU
ISLAND

SOUTH
MANITOU
ISLAND

LIGHTHOUSE

I MANITOU
SHOAL LIGHT
"The Crib"

MANITOU
PASSAGE

MANITOU
PASSAGE

N

MANITOU
PASSAGE

PYRAMID
POINT

Good Harbor Bay

To Leland

Hidden Lake

Lake Michigan Rd.

Shell Lake

Narada Lake

Narada Creek

Bass Lake

M-22

School Lake

Little Traverse Lake

School Lake Rd.

Lime Lake

C-651

C-667

C-669

PORT   ONEIDA
RURAL HISTORIC DISTRICT

M-22

Sleeping
Bear
Bay

Sleeping
Bear
Point

GLEN
HAVEN

GLEN
ARBOR

Darwin Rd.

Jucker Lake

Miller Hill Rd.

Wheeler Rd.

MARITIME
MUSEUM

THE
SLEEPING
BEAR

DUNE
CLIMB

PIERCE
STOCKING
DRIVE

M-109

Stocking Rd.

M-109

M-109

Crystal River

Fisher Lake

Big
Glen
Lake

Little
Glen
Lake

Day Forest Rd.

Trumbel Rd.

Tremain Rd.

C-675

MAPLE
CITY

C-616

CEDAR

C-651

C-616

BURDICKVILLE

C-675

C-669

North
Bar Lake

South
Bar Lake

Voice Rd.

M-22

EMPIRE

M-72

M-72

To Traverse City

LEELANAU   COUNTY
BENZIE   COUNTY

EMPIRE
BLUFFS

M-22

Miller Rd.

LAKE MICHIGAN

Platte Bay

Esch Rd.

Otter Creek

C-610

C-677

Otter
Lake

Trails End Rd.

Bass
Lake

Deer
Lake

PLATTE RIVER
POINT

PETERSON
BEACH

Lake Michigan Rd.

Peterson Rd.

Platte River

C-679

PYRAMID PT.
TRAIL HEAD

LAURA
BASCH
FARM

Manitou
Passage

Port Oneida Rd.

Baker Rd.

BASCH
FARM

BURFIELD
FARM

WERNER
CEMETERY

Kelderhouse Rd.

Narada
Lake

MILLER
BARN

Miller Rd.

DECHOW
KLETT FARM

M-22

Sutter Rd.

Basch Rd.

Wheeler Rd.

C-610

THORESON
FARM

Thoreson Rd.

M-22

PORT   ONEIDA
RURAL HISTORIC DISTRICT

Baekelo Rd.

Loon
Lake

Suter Rd.

To Frankfort

Long Lake

Round Lake

Warren Rd.

Rush Lake

Deadstream Rd.

Little
Platte
Lake

Platte
Lake

C-708

C-706

US 31

HONOR

Crystal Lake

C-704

BENZIE COUNTY
GRAND TRAVERSE COUNTY

Views *from the* Sleeping Bear

PHOTOGRAPHS OF THE SLEEPING BEAR DUNES NATIONAL LAKESHORE

THOMAS KACHADURIAN

Library of Congress Cataloging-in-Publication Data
Kachadurian, Thomas.
View from the Sleeping Bear: photographs of the Sleeping Bear Dunes National Lakeshore / Thomas Kachadurian.
p.   cm.
ISBN 1-886947-37-6
1. Sleeping Bear Dunes National Lakeshore (Mich.)--Pictorial works. I. Kachadurian, Thomas. II. Title.
F572.S8K33 1998
977. 4'635--dc21

Sleeping Bear Press
121 South Main
P.O. Box 20
Chelsea, MI 48118
www.sleepingbearpress.com

Printed and bound in Canada.

10 9 8 7 6 5 4 3 2 1

FOR MY FATHER, HARRY H. KACHADURIAN

He gave me my first camera and the self-confidence to use it.

FOREWORD

The people of Michigan have been blessed with countless natural resources. One of our greatest gifts, the Sleeping Bear Dunes, has drawn visitors for over a century. The towering sand dunes and the crystal blue water of Lake Michigan are treasures we all cherish.

This book celebrates the power of the waves thundering at the Lake Michigan shore as well as the grace of dune grass bending in the breeze. These photographs capture more than a view. They reveal those things that we all carry in our hearts—the memories of summer vacations that warm our winters, and the sounds of spring hikes that fill quiet moments. The images recall a slower time—from farm life as it was in the Port Oneida region to ageless voices of children playing on the beach.

Thomas Kachadurian shares his passion for the Sleeping Bear Dunes through his photographs and his words. His work reveals a respect for the land and water that teaches us all to honor the great gifts we have so near to our homes. Through his work, Kachadurian invites us all to protect and preserve this place, to keep it unspoiled now and for all generations to come.

—William G. Milliken
Former Governor of Michigan

PREFACE

The Sleeping Bear Dunes National Lakeshore has certain boundaries, and can be described on a plat map. But the legal boundaries don't accurately mark the perceived area of the park. Instead, it is our experiences that define the Lakeshore. For some it is a system of trails, each leading to new, yet familiar vistas. At the park's southernmost boundary, the Old Indian Trail leads to sand dunes that sweep out in modest waves. They reveal the contours of the moraines beneath the sand—ridges and hills of gravel left by the receding glaciers. There are private homes south of the park's boundaries, yet those residents certainly consider themselves part of the Sleeping Bear Dunes National Lakeshore.

Some tourists stop only at the Dune Climb, assuming, mistakenly, that they are climbing the Sleeping Bear. The Sleeping Bear herself is nearly gone now, the dune slowly carved into a bowl by the constant winds coming in off Lake Michigan.

While making this manuscript I talked to hundreds of people, residents of the Lakeshore, National Park employees, and tourists. I have included some of their ideas as well as my own. The photographs in this book are mostly made from or near public trails and access areas in or near the Sleeping Bear Dunes National Lakeshore. These are the places and experiences we all can share.

PYRAMID POINT, DAWN

As the sun lies at the horizon, the dunes rise gold from the shoreline. A wind blows cold off the open water, making a July morning feel like November. The sky changes slowly from muddy grey to shades of violet, then deeper purples, and finally to brilliant blue. The sand flows down from the top of Pyramid Point, like a river of platinum into Lake Michigan. The lake stretches across to the Manitou Islands, which come into such clear view that The Crib east of North Manitou looks like a child's toy that you could reach down and pick up. Only the white dot of the South Manitou Light reveals the true distance.

The sun seems eager to reach its apex, and rises so quickly from the horizon that you can see it move in the sky. Warmed by the sun, the dew-covered sand dries in patches before it's even 7:00 in the morning. You are alone. It will be hours before any other hikers make their way up the trail from Port Oneida Road. You lie down on the sand, now warm to the touch, and sleep; and in sleep, you dream.

In sleep your struggles—work, a house that needs attention, family conflicts—merge with the climb up the steep wall of sand. These dreams mingle with visions of a great mother bear frantically swimming across Lake Michigan in a storm, trying to pull her cubs beside her. Her strength fades with each wave that crashes over her head, trying to take her under. She only realizes that she's lost her grip on her children when she gets to the shore and falls down, spent. The great bear looks up only to see that the spirit Manitou has lifted her cubs from the water, and holds them safely above it. Relieved and exhausted, she sleeps next to you, and in her dreams the cubs dance across the water, their steps safe and firm above its surface. You join her in a deep sleep. All problems fall away and the waves and wind rock you as your mother's arms once did. The sun warms away the chill and you open your eyes to the full blaze of morning. The wind off the lake blows the sleep from your eyes, and before you turn to head back down the trail, you fill your lungs with clear air, scented with the mist of cool water.

At dawn, alone at the top of a dune, or at dusk around a beach fire, we begin to know the great bear. From Lake Michigan's cool waters to the solitude of hidden lakes and trails, countless personal discoveries have unfolded and still more wait to be revealed. And like the sand, constantly moving and changing, our experiences and memories are molded by the Lakeshore. We each have our own Sleeping Bear.

ON THE COVER: PLATTE RIVER AT LAKE MICHIGAN.
PAGE 6: BEACH AT EMPIRE, VIEW TO SLEEPING BEAR DUNES.
PAGES 7 AND 8: PYRAMID POINT.
OPPOSITE: OLD SETTLER'S PARK, BIG GLEN LAKE.

OPPOSITE: PIERCE STOCKING SCENIC DRIVE, VIEW SOUTH TO EMPIRE.
ABOVE: SLEEPING BEAR POINT.

ABOVE: GLEN HAVEN.
OPPOSITE: STEELHEAD FISHING, SHALDA CREEK.

OPPOSITE: EMPIRE, VIEW FROM EMPIRE BLUFF HIKING AND SKI TRAIL.

THE BEACH AT BOEKELODGE

North of the Old Indian Trailhead, along M-22, Boekeloo Road turns west toward Lake Michigan. The narrow gravel road winds through the trees for more than a mile, then ends abruptly at a cul-de-sac, where there is a metal gate and a sign asking you not to block it. Hidden behind the trees just west of the parking area is the Boekelodge, a private residence that will revert to park ownership in the twenty-first century.

The lodge, really more of a log cottage, faces a tiny island in the middle of a modest pond. North of the Boekelodge, a path leads west toward Lake Michigan. The path starts in dense woods, then disappears into open sand and dune grass. Unlike the Old Indian Trail, just south of Boekeloo Road, there isn't a dramatic climb up a hill to a sweeping view. Here the sand rolls out, covering the moraines in small hills and valleys for hundreds of yards. Climbing the modest inclines will never take your breath. Still, the small valleys hide microswamps, some just ten yards across, and other tiny ecosystems.

Finally, after you've hiked up and down sand dunes for the last quarter of a mile, Lake Michigan beckons. On a windy day the waves thunder at the shore as the weather moves in, unchallenged, from Wisconsin. When the lake is calm, the beach here is exceptionally quiet. The long walk is never challenging, which makes this an ideal beach for bathers seeking seclusion rather than adventure. There may be others sharing the beach, but it stretches so far north and south that privacy is no farther than the next small dune.

The hike back to the parking area seems much shorter than the hike to the beach. A small handmade box is attached to the exterior door of the Boekelodge. You can leave the Boekeloo family a note and tell them how much you have enjoyed this part of the Lakeshore that bears their name.

Pond at Boekelodge.

ABOVE: OLD INDIAN HIKING AND SKI TRAIL.
OPPOSITE: COTTONWOOD TRAIL, PIERCE STOCKING SCENIC DRIVE.

OPPOSITE: PLATTE RIVER AT LAKE MICHIGAN.

OPPOSITE: EMPIRE BLUFF HIKING AND SKI TRAIL.

MARKING THE PAST

One of the discoveries to be made in the Sleeping Bear Dunes National Lakeshore is the Werner Cemetery, hidden along a ridge in Port Oneida. Before I knew to look for it, I hiked the narrow path many times, through the trees and past the small fenced plot. Although it is less than ten feet from the footpath, I never noticed it.

To find the cemetery, hike east from the parking area at the end of Miller Road, off Port Oneida Road. Stay to the north edge of the clearing just east of the Miller barn and walk toward the shore. Nearly at the ridge line there is a footpath between the trees. Take the path north through the trees (as you face the water, north is to your right). The century-old Werner Cemetery is hidden in the forest about 300 yards from where the path first enters the trees. The grave markers, many of them in German, tell the story of the immigrant settlers to the region. Artificial flowers left behind show that these early homesteaders still have family in the area today.

At the cemetery another path leads down the steep hill to the shoreline. While it isn't exactly dangerous, the narrow, sloping path can be tricky, and the same beach is just a short walk south along the shore from South Lane Road.

Continuing north along the path leads to an overlook just above South Lane Road. Locals call this spot "Lookout Point," but you won't find it on any trail map. The National Park Service has named another area along the Farms Trail "Lookout Point," and often people looking for the cemetery end up behind the Miller barn near the Park Service's lookout point.

The hike from the Miller barn to the cemetery isn't always easy, but anyone accustomed to moderate walking will not be challenged. The cemetery, a place of quiet reverence nestled in the woods, is an exhilarating discovery.

PAGE 27 AND ABOVE: WERNER CEMETERY, PORT ONEIDA RURAL HISTORIC DISTRICT.
OPPOSITE: NORTH BAR LAKE.

OPPOSITE: WETLAND, PORT ONEIDA.

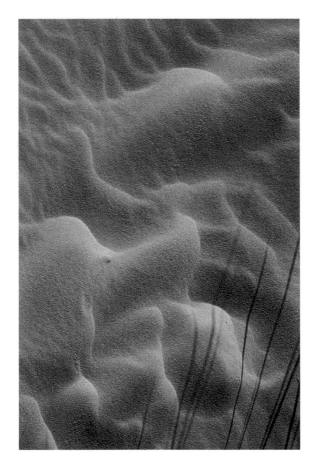

OPPOSITE: PYRAMID POINT.

LEFT: MARTIN BASCH FARM, PORT ONEIDA RURAL HISTORIC DISTRICT.

OPPOSITE: CHARLES OLSEN FARM, PORT ONEIDA RURAL HISTORIC DISTRICT.
ABOVE: FOOT TRAIL OFF GREENAN ROAD.

SUNNY SWANSON'S

One morning last September, after photographing some pumpkins in front of Sunny Swanson's barn, I returned to where I parked my car to find Sunny and his wife. They were deeply concerned, not that I was on their property, nor that I was photographing their barn. They hadn't seen me walk down the path early that morning, and were worried that my car had been abandoned the night before. Since no one had come to their door in the night, they were concerned that the car's owner had wandered into the woods and was in trouble. They were relieved to find everyone safe from harm.

Sunny Swanson is from a different era. He is the proprietor of the small yellow fruit stand along M-22 across from Sugar Loaf Road. He still farms today on the plot that was his father's, offering produce at his roadside concession adjacent to the front door of his house. You can't do your weekly shopping there. Sunny only has the vegetables and fruits he grows himself, only the things he picks each day when they are ready to be eaten. Sometimes in August there's corn sold within the hour it's picked. Late in summer the apricots are still warm from the sun that has ripened them on the tree to a juicy sweetness. Sunny's accounting relies on a spiral notebook where you write down your purchases and a coffee can where you put your money.

I cherish each meeting I have with Sunny. I am grateful for tomatoes that have never been in storage. I'm relieved that someone still has enough faith in people to use the honor system. I am impressed with the diplomacy Sunny employs when a cottager passing by isn't satisfied with the selection.

"Do you have these in orange?" she asks, pointing to some red and yellow gladioli.

"No, just those today," Sunny says. "I had some pink ones this morning."

"Will you have any tomorrow?"

"I'll have more pink ones tomorrow."

"But no orange ones."

"Well, I could plant some for you next year. I'll have pink tomorrow."

In an article on Sunny published in 1994, he said he expected to stop farming in a year or two. Four years later, at 77, Sunny is still there each morning putting out the fresh produce. It seems he'll be farming for a while, but he is a quiet man, and there won't be any ceremony when a summer comes and he doesn't put out the coffee can and ledger. For me and countless others, that will be a sad day.

SUNNY'S FRUIT STAND, M-22.

OPPOSITE: SUNNY'S FRUIT STAND, M-22.
ABOVE: EMPIRE AND THE SLEEPING BEAR DUNES, VIEW FROM EMPIRE BLUFFS.

ABOVE: M-109, VIEW NORTH TO GLEN ARBOR.
OPPOSITE: LITTLE GLEN LAKE.

OTTER LAKE, AUGUST

 Although I know it's there, I nearly drive past Trail's End Road. I'm heading south from Empire along M-22 and the road hides around a sharp corner. I head west down Trail's End Road and past the canoe landing at Otter Lake to where the road ends at the Platte Plains Trail head. This summer evening there is a family fishing in Bass Lake (one of several so named in the region). Two parents cast from the small dock, while a teenaged boy and girl cast from shore just out of earshot of the parents. It isn't clear which of the teens has selected this location, but it is clearly a supervised date. The boy is more interested in fishing, however, and doesn't notice the the adoring glances from his companion.

Another man drags a small flat-bottomed boat from the back of his pickup truck to water's edge. The launch here is a place where a car can be parked to unload; there is no boat ramp. He loads fishing equipment and two small girls into the boat and pushes off from the shore just as the moon rises in the east.

I hike from the parking area back up the now-closed portion of Trail's End Road that once followed the south side of Otter Creek. I hear a single loon calling in the distance, and find a clearing to the north. Otter Lake is usually the summer home to a nesting pair of loons, but this late in the summer the chicks have grown and are venturing out on their own. The call is from a mother loon, circling the shore, calling her children home. She sees me at the bank and moves slowly. Her concern for her young has waned with the summer, and when her call gets no answer she paddles delicately back toward her nest across the lake, and comfortably away from me. With the sun low in the sky the water turns to glass, reflecting the trees along the shoreline. I make a few photographs and head back to the trail.

OPPOSITE: OTTER CREEK, AT LAKE MICHIGAN.

OPPOSITE: THE BEACH AT PYRAMID POINT.
ABOVE: NORTH BAR LAKE AND EMPIRE BLUFF.

A HIDDEN LAKE

Lake Michigan Road turns west off Leelanau County Road 669 where it ends at Lake Michigan. The dusty road winds past Shalda Creek and into the woods. It turns back toward the shoreline and ends just east of Pyramid Point, near Hidden Lake. You won't read about the aptly-named Hidden Lake in a guidebook. The official map from the National Park Service doesn't show roads or even water there. In fact, it is difficult to find any written reference to the tiny lake at all.

Explorers who take the first right at the fork in Lake Michigan Road, following their instincts to hug the shoreline, will end up at a secluded beach, but will still be a mile east of Pyramid Point. The left fork, however, leads deeper into the woods where the road itself becomes crooked and narrow until it ends at a dirt parking area. An overgrown two-track at the north side of the parking area leads through an open meadow, then twists into the woods. As it turns back toward the shore, the path gets so narrow at places that larger vehicles will be brushed on both sides by trees. Often seasonal rainfall will turn the road into a series of nearly impassable mud holes. When the two-track reaches the Lake Michigan shore, it takes one more final turn west. This last stretch of road, less than a quarter of a mile, is often best traveled on foot. The road finally ends at a sandy parking area at the base of Pyramid Point. From here hikers can choose three paths.

This remote area is usually sought by sunbathers, so the path most traveled leads north to the beach below Pyramid Point. Another path to the west slopes so sharply upward that climbing the soft sand is nearly impossible and will only lead to further erosion and damage to the vegetation. Another foot trail is so well veiled by shade that people who have been there dozens of times don't know the path exists.

This small foot trail disappears into the woods south of the parking area. In the woods, fallen trees frequently block the way until the path opens to the side of a grassy dune. A trail switches back and forth up the side of the dune to a ridge high above the water. A look to the east reveals the only clear view of Hidden Lake nestled just below the ridge. The hills of Sugar Loaf Resort are visible farther east. Whaleback, the low dune near Leland, lies northeast, and North Manitou Island seems so near in the north that the Manitou Shoals Lighthouse ("The Crib") looks no more than a stone's throw away.

ABOVE: SUNSET ROAD BEACH.
OPPOSITE: SHALDA CREEK.

OPPOSITE: THE DUNE CLIMB.

60

OPPOSITE: LAKE MICHIGAN BEACH AT OTTER CREEK.
ABOVE: BIG GLEN LAKE, VIEW FROM INSPIRATION POINT.

ABOVE: D. H. DAY FARM.
OPPOSITE: PLATTE RIVER.

LAKE MICHIGAN, VIEW FROM LOOKOUT POINT, BAY VIEW HIKING AND SKI TRAIL.

THE BEACH AT GLEN ARBOR.

OPPOSITE: PIERCE STOCKING SCENIC DRIVE, NEAR THE SLEEPING BEAR DUNE.

OPPOSITE: THE COTTONWOOD TRAIL, VIEW TO SOUTH MANITOU ISLAND.
ABOVE: EMPIRE BEACH, VIEW TO EMPIRE BLUFF.

SLEEPING BEAR POINT, JULY

Sleeping Bear Point is a quiet place, perhaps busiest when a few families from Glen Arbor hike down the trail to play capture-the-flag between the dunes. Even on peak July days there are rarely more than five cars in the parking area near the Maritime Museum. In the early morning Sleeping Bear Point is abandoned.

It is still night when I park my car at the trailhead. The sky is just beginning to glow, but under the cover of trees, it's so dark that I can't see more than a few feet in front of me. As the trail opens out into the dunes, the sand reflects just enough of the predawn light to illuminate shapes without detail. The dunes that rise up to my right look like a selenium-toned black-and-white photograph. I hike along the dune ridge bordered on one side by trees, and just beyond them, Glen Haven. I look down the other side of the ridge and see the sand sweeping out into a series of dunes, creating trails with their valleys. Except for two blue- tipped trail markers more than a mile away, and a barely distinguishable freighter several miles out in the Manitou Passage, there is no sign of human life.

I hike along the ridge to a sheer bluff that drops 200 feet to the water. The water level is 30 inches above normal this year, so high that after a windy night, no footprints remain on the beach below. First there are small slivers of light on South Manitou Island, and then, in an instant, the sun reveals itself on the horizon. Slices of gold sand ignite the top of each dune, turning the flat purple landscape into a dramatic pattern of dark and light. Minutes later the sun is filling the valleys with deep shadows. In this first light, blades of dune grass cast seven-foot shadows, like dancers with their arms gracefully arched to their sides.

The overnight wind has erased any footprints, leaving gently flowing waves of sand that stretch out for miles. I hike further along the trail until I get to the ghost trees in the valley near Devil's Hole. Although they are the last traces of a forest, the bare trunks—carved to points by years of abrasion—seem to shoot straight up like alien vegetation. It will be an hour, perhaps several, before any other hikers make their way along this trail. At the bottom of a small valley, protected from the wind on three sides, I sit to rest. In every direction there is nothing but sand and sky. Even Lake Michigan is hidden from view. For a brief moment I can easily imagine that I am on another planet.

PAGE 90 AND 91: DUNES-SLEEPING BEAR POINT HIKING TRAIL.

PORT ONEIDA, DAYBREAK

 On a clear moonlit night the Barratt pig barn glows. I can see it clearly from the bluff just north of the Werner Cemetery. When the full moon sets in the west, just before daybreak, it provides enough light to guide me across the open field where the town of Port Oneida once stood. As I head east, the Burfiend farm moves into shadow and coyotes howl.

First there is one faint bark that sounds like a stray dog. Then, in minutes, the skin on the back of my neck turns cold with the sound of dozens of howling voices. I can't see the wild dogs hiding deep in the swamp beyond the Barratt property, but they sound near as I cross Port Oneida Road. There isn't enough light yet for my photograph, so I listen to the dogs. I set up my tripod as loudly as I can, just to let them know I'm here.

As I finish setting up my camera, a single dark cloud passes under the moon and for a few minutes I can't see my own hands. The coyotes are suddenly quiet, which is more alarming than their howls. I struggle to see anything in the silent darkness. Then, in an instant, I hear the sound of birds. The pig barn's peaked roof reaches up to the first light that creeps over the horizon. Fog begins to form off the warm mist of the swamp and wraps itself around the barn. In the growing daylight I can see that I am close to the edge of the swamp, which is just a few feet to my right. I expose two frames, and before I can make a third photograph, the barn is completely obscured by fog. My shooting for the morning is over.

Barratt Pig Barn, Port Oneida Rural Historic District.

OPPOSITE: CANNERY BOAT MUSEUM, GLEN HAVEN.

PORT ONEIDA RURAL HISTORIC DISTRICT.
PAGE 101: MARTIN BASCH FARM.
OPPOSITE: MILLER BARN.
ABOVE: BURFIEND FARM.

PORT ONEIDA RURAL HISTORIC DISTRICT.
OPPOSITE: BURFIEND FARM.
ABOVE: MARTIN BASCH FARM.

OPPOSITE: PIERCE STOCKING SCENIC DRIVE, #10 OVERLOOK, VIEW TO EMPIRE BLUFF.
ABOVE: BURFIEND FARM, PORT ONEIDA RURAL HISTORIC DISTRICT.

PAGE 108: SLEEPING BEAR POINT, VIEW TO SOUTH MANITOU ISLAND.
PAGE 109: PYRAMID POINT VIEW TO NORTH MANITOU ISLAND.
OPPOSITE: LASSO LOOP, PLATTE PLAINS HIKING AND SKI TRIAL.
ABOVE: PLATTE RIVER AT LAKE MICHIGAN.

ABOVE: GLEN HAVEN BEACH.
OPPOSITE: SAND SLIDE, PYRAMID POINT, 1998.

ABOVE BIG GLEN

Many have marveled at the view from Miller Hill. The trees have been cleared down one side of Miller Hill to make room for power lines, creating a dramatic vista of Big Glen Lake. A less obstructed view is available for those who are willing to hike through the woods. South on Miller Hill Road, about 500 yards from the power line turnout, there is a tiny clearing, marked only by small brown logs, intended to keep off-road vehicles from the trail. Parking is tight, but a car can be left along the road's edge while still leaving room for the few cars that might pass by. The trail into and through the woods leads to a ridge above the tree line that has been cleared.

From the clearing, all of Big Glen is visible. Beyond Big Glen, the narrows, Little Glen, and dunes sweep into the distance. Fisher Lake is so close below that the laughter of children playing in the water can be heard clearly. Beyond the inland lakes, Sleeping Bear Point stretches into the west. It is a difficult trail to identify, but the view is a handsome reward for the search.

PAGE 116: SAND SLIDE, PYRAMID POINT, 1998.
PAGE 117: NARADA SWAMP.
ABOVE: LITTLE GLEN LAKE, VIEW TO THE DUNE CLIMB.
OVERLEAF: SLEEPING BEAR POINT, VIEW FROM MILLER HILL.

THE COTTONWOOD TRAIL, PIERCE STOCKING SCENIC DRIVE.

BURFIEND FARM, PORT ONEIDA RURAL HISTORIC DISTRICT.

ABOVE: THE DUNE CLIMB.
OPPOSITE: GLEN HAVEN BEACH.

AT EMPIRE BEACH

With the sun low on the horizon I park my trailer at the boat launch at South Bar Lake. It's really more of a canoe landing, so only the lightest boats can be launched here. Rather than risk getting the trailer stuck in the soft sand, I pull and lift the boat off the trailer and into the water.

As I push off from the shore I can hear children shouting on the swings in the play area. The sounds of the waves crashing on the Lake Michigan shore are louder than my oars as I move north through the water. The crashing waves and the voices fade as I float slowly north. The dense swamp grasses and wild flowers on the western shore block the parking area from my view. So much of the Sleeping Bear Dunes National Lakeshore is secluded that it's easy to forget the charm of its public places. Floating on South Bar there is a blend of quiet, punctuated by the comforting sounds of a teenage girl laughing and, now and again, a car door slamming.

As the sky turns pale pink and details on the west shore become silhouetted, the panfish begin to break the surface. I cast a tiny rubber spider toward the grass on the east bank and a bluegill responds almost instantly with a "snap" on the water's surface. The small fish puts a nice bow in my 3-weight rod as I bring him in and then let him go. For the next hour I catch and release several others. These aren't trophy fish, most of them no bigger than my hand. But fishing is just a way to pass the time while I watch the sky change from pink to orange, then to crimson and to blue.

The fish stop feeding as abruptly as they started. I pack up my fly rod and begin to row toward the launch. The parking area is almost empty now. There are a few cars left from people who are lingering on the beach after dark. I hear my oars in the water and in the distance, Lori Carson on a car stereo singing:

It's hard to take for granted
This gold light
These cool nights
It's kind of fall again
And this is our life.

I pull my boat up to the shore of South Bar and walk across the road to the Lake Michigan Beach. The waves on the open water seem to be losing their strength, but the breeze still cools the late summer air, foretelling the colder weather soon to come. Among the rocks I find a spot of soft sand, and I sit to watch a freighter on the horizon. It's always too early for an evening like this to end.

SOUTH BAR LAKE.

ABOVE: Lake Michigan overlook, Pierce Stocking Scenic Drive.
OPPOSITE: Coast Guard Museum, Glen Haven.

SOUTH BAR LAKE

PLATTE RIVER.

ABOVE: BEACH AT GLEN ARBOR, JULY 4, 1997.
OPPOSITE: PLATTE RIVER AT LAKE MICHIGAN.
PAGE 142: LAURA BASCH FARM, PORT ONEIDA RURAL HISTORIC DISTRICT.
PAGE 143: PIERCE STOCKING SCENIC DRIVE, VIEW TO THE SLEEPING BEAR.

A NOTE ON THE PHOTOGRAPHS

Photography is an art that relies on science. While I do not profess to be an expert on technical photography, I include the following data for those who hope to improve their own work by understanding the methods of others.

With rare exception, these images were made on Fujichrome Velvia in 35mm and 120 rolls and 4x5 sheets. They were processed in small batches with a Jobo CPP-2 Rotary Processor. I have not included exposure data because my calibrations are based on my meter and processing method, and will have little relevance for any other photographer. My exposures were based on incident and reflected readings from Sekonic and Minolta meters.

No enhancing or warming filters were used, except for polarizers, which I used often to reveal the colors and depth of the water. I relied instead on the changing hues of morning and evening light to create the many moods reflected in these photographs.

The following list details which lens I used to make each photograph. As the list reveals, nearly 20 different lenses and 6 different cameras were used to make these photographs. Still, the bulk were made with a 50mm lens on a Mamiya 6; 50mm and 28mm lenses on a Leica M4-P and a 300mm lens on a Canon EOS A2.

All but a handful of these photographs were made with the camera on a tripod, probably my most important photographic tool.

PHOTOGRAPH INFORMATION

Page	Camera	Lens	Page	Camera	Lens	Page	Camera	Lens
cover	Mamiya 6	50mm f4.0	51	Mamiya 6	50mm f4.0	99	Mamiya 6	50mm f4.0
5	Leica M4-P	90mm Tele-Elmarit-M	52	Mamiya 6	50mm f4.0	101	Wista DX	90mm f8.0 Super Angulon
6	Mamiya 6	50mm f4.0	53	Mamiya 645	150mm f3.5	102	Wista DX	90mm f8.0 Super Angulon
7	Canon EOS A2	EF 24mm f2.8	55	Mamiya 6	150mm f4.5	103	Mamiya 6	50mm f4.0
8	Mamiya 6	50mm f4.0	56	Mamiya 6	50mm f4.0	104	Mamiya 6	50mm f4.0
10	Canon EOS A2	EF 300mm f4.0L / 25mm EX tube	57	Mamiya 6	50mm f4.0	105	Mamiya 645	45mm f2.8
11	Mamiya 6	50mm f4.0	58	Mamiya 6	50mm f4.0	106	Mamiya 6	50mm f4.0
12	Mamiya 6	50mm f4.0	59	Mamiya 6	150mm f4.5	107	Nikon FE-2	24mm f2.8
13	Leica M4-P	28mm f2.8 Rokkor-M	60	Leica M4-P	28mm f2.8 Rokkor-M	108	Mamiya 6	50mm f4.0
14	Canon EOS A2	EF 300mm f4.0L	61	Mamiya 6	75mm f3.5	109	Mamiya 6	50mm f4.0
15	Mamiya 6	50mm f4.0	62	Canon EOS A2	EF 300mm f4.0L	110	Mamiya 6	50mm f4.0
16	Mamiya 6	150mm f4.5	63	Wista DX	150mm Fujinon f5.6 N	111	Mamiya 6	50mm f4.0
17	Canon EOS A2	EF 300mm f4.0L / 25mm EX tube	64	Mamiya 6	50mm f4.0	112	Mamiya 6	50mm f4.0
19	Canon EOS A2	EF 100mm f2.0	65	Wista DX	90mm f8.0 Super Angulon	113	Nikon F4s	AF 85mm f1.8
20	Mamiya 6	50mm f4.0	66	Mamiya 6	75mm f3.5	114	Mamiya 6	50mm f4.0
21	Mamiya 6	50mm f4.0	67	Mamiya 6	50mm f4.0	115	Mamiya 6	50mm f4.0
22	Mamiya 645	150mm f3.5	69	Canon EOS A2	EF 50mm f1.4	116	Mamiya 6	50mm f4.0
23	Mamiya 6	50mm f4.0	70	Mamiya 6	75mm f3.5	117	Mamiya 6	50mm f4.0
24	Canon EOS A2	EF 300mm f4.0L / 25mm EX tube	71	Canon EOS A2	EF 300mm f4.0L	119	Canon EOS A2	EF 300mm f4.0L
25	Mamiya 6	50mm f4.0	72	Leica M4-P	50mm Summicron-M	120	Mamiya 6	150mm f4.5
27	Mamiya 6	50mm f4.0	73	Leica M4-P	90mm Tele-Elmarit-M	122	Canon EOS A2	EF 300mm f4.0L /12mm EX tube
28	Mamiya 6	75mm f3.5	74	Mamiya 6	50mm f4.0	123	Mamiya 6	50mm f4.0
29	Mamiya 6	50mm f4.0	75	Mamiya 6	50mm f4.0	124	Mamiya 6	50mm f4.0
30	Mamiya 6	50mm f4.0	76	Mamiya 6	50mm f4.0	125	Canon EOS A2	EF 300mm f4.0L
31	Canon EOS A2	EF 300mm f4.0L / 12mm EX tube	77	Canon EOS A2	EF 300mm f4.0L	127	Wista DX	90mm f8.0 Super Angulon
32	Leica M4-P	50mm Summicron-M	78	Leica M4-P	50mm Summicron-M	128	Mamiya 6	50mm f4.0
33	Mamiya 6	150mm f4.5	79	Canon EOS A2	EF 24mm f2.8	129	Mamiya 6	50mm f4.0
34	Wista DX	150mm Fujinon f5.6 N	81	Mamiya 6	50mm f4.0	130	Mamiya 645	45mm f2.8
35	Canon EOS A2	EF 300mm f4.0L / 12mm EX tube	82	Mamiya 6	50mm f4.0	131	Wista DX	150mm Fujinon f5.6 N
36	Canon EOS A2	EF 24mm f2.8	83	Nikon F4s	AF 180mm f2.8	132	Mamiya 6	50mm f4.0
37	Mamiya 6	50mm f4.0	84	Canon EOS A2	EF 300mm f4.0L with 12mm EX tube	133	Mamiya 6	50mm f4.0
39	Mamiya 6	50mm f4.0	85	Mamiya 6	75mm f3.5	135	Canon EOS A2	EF 50mm f1.4
40	Mamiya 6	50mm f4.0	86	Mamiya 6	50mm f4.0	136	Leica M4-P	28mm f2.8 Rokkor-M
41	Canon EOS A2	EF 300mm f4.0L	87	Mamiya 6	75mm f3.5	137	Mamiya 6	50mm f4.0
42	Leica M4-P	50mm Summicron-M	89	Mamiya 6	50mm f4.0	138	Canon EOS A2	EF 300mm f4.0L
43	Mamiya 6	50mm f4.0	90	Mamiya 6	50mm f4.0	139	Canon EOS A2	EF 300mm f4.0L
44	Leica M4-P	90mm Tele-Elmarit-M	91	Leica M4-P	28mm f2.8 Rokkor-M	140	Canon EOS A2	EF 24mm f2.8
45	Leica M4-P	90mm Tele-Elmarit-M	92	Canon EOS A2	EF 100mm f2.0	141	Mamiya 6	50mm f4.0
46	Canon EOS A2	EF 300mm f4.0L	93	Mamiya 6	75mm f3.5	142	Mamiya 6	50mm f4.0
47	Mamiya 6	50mm f4.0	95	Canon EOS A2	EF 300mm f4.0L	143	Leica M4-P	28mm f2.8 Rokkor-M
48	Mamiya 6	75mm f3.5	96	Canon EOS A2	EF 300mm f4.0L			
49	Leica M4-P	50mm Summicron-M	97	Canon EOS A2	EF 300mm f4.0L			
50	Leica M4-P	90mm Tele-Elmarit-M	98	Mamiya 6	150mm f4.5			